# Historic Inns *of the* Northeast

**CRESCENT BOOKS**
New York

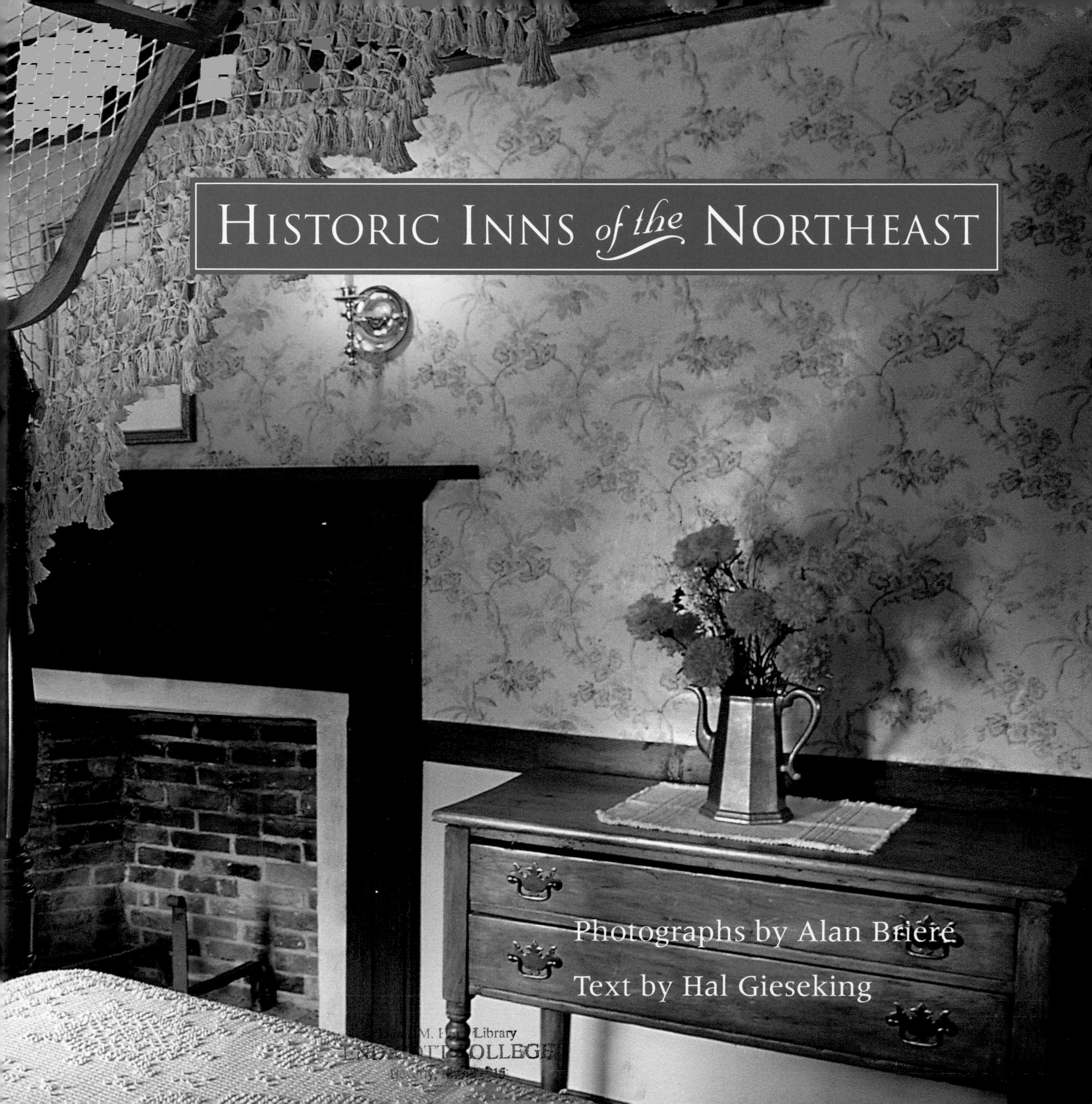

# Historic Inns *of the* Northeast

Photographs by Alan Brieré

Text by Hal Gieseking

This 1992 edition was published by Crescent Books, distributed by Outlet Book Company, Inc., a Random House Company, 225 Park Avenue South, New York, New York 10003

Printed and bound in Hong Kong
ISBN 0-517-05666-6
8 7 6 5 4 3 2 1

*Historic Inns of the Northeast* was prepared and produced by Moore & Moore Publishing, 11 W. 19th Street, New York, New York 10011

**Previous pages** Nathaniel Porter Inn, Warren, Rhode Island
**These pages** White Goose Inn, Orford, New Hampshire
**Page 128** The Charlotte Inn, Edgartown, Massachusetts

AN M&M BOOK
**Project Director & Editor** Gary Fishgall

**Editorial Assistants** Maxine Dormer, Ben D'Amprisi, Jr.
**Copy Editing** Bert N. Zelman and Keith Walsh of Publishers Workshop Inc.

**Designer** Marcy Stamper

**Separations and Printing** Regent Publishing Services Ltd.

# Contents

# Introduction

THERE IS NOTHING WHICH HAS YET BEEN CONTRIVED BY MAN, BY WHICH SO MUCH HAPPINESS IS PRODUCED AS BY A GOOD TAVERN OR INN.

Samuel Johnson, *Celebrated English writer and conversationalist*

DOWN THROUGH THE AGES, many travelers who found shelter along the road would have agreed with Samuel Johnson.

There have been inns almost from the beginning of recorded history. In the days of the Roman Empire, merchants and tax collectors rested at early versions called mansiones. In the 13th century Marco Polo found a well-developed system of trailside inns in China. Monasteries of the Middle Ages offered cold travelers blanket space around a fire and a hot bowl from the common pot.

The English refined the art of innkeeping, introducing comfortable lodging space; tables covered with roasts, breads, and vegetables; and musical entertainment. These inns spread to the new British colonies in America and later leapfrogged across the new nation along the paths of stagecoaches, canals, and eventually trains and automobiles.

This book will introduce you to some of the most historic inns of the Northeast, all still welcoming travelers. The oldest structure is the Daggett House in Martha's Vineyard, Massachusetts, started in 1660. The "youngest" is the Juniper Hill Inn, constructed in 1902 in Windsor, Vermont.

Many of the inns are woven into the warp and woof of American life. Their construction dates become even more meaningful when related to events occurring elsewhere in the United States as they were being built. In the 1850s, for example, when farmers were raising a house that eventually became the Old Lyme Inn in Connecticut, many other people were racing westward to join the great California Gold Rush. In 1869, as the Abbey was being built in Cape May, New Jersey, John Wesley Powell was struggling to become the first white American to navigate the Colorado River through the Grand Canyon.

But American history is more than headline-making events. It is the compendium of many commonplace occurrences in the lives of ordinary people. We'll refer to some of these milestones as well in order to place the origination of our inns in a larger context. For example, in 1882, as workers hoisted logs into place for the lodge that became Lake Placid Manor in the Adirondacks of New York, William Horlick in Racine, Wisconsin, was inventing a new kind of ice cream drink, the malted milk. In 1897, when the Victorian Bechtel Mansion was being erected in East Berlin, Pennsylvania, workers in Boston were installing the rails for America's first subway trains.

These historic inns are thus part of the fabric of our national past. By their architecture and design they are also "snapshots" of their eras, mortar-frame-and-brick museums of Colonial, Federal, Empire, Victorian, and Beaux Arts styles. Unlike so many modern hotel rooms stamped from the same "cookie cutter" design, the inns' chambers are filled with antiques and eclectic surprises.

This book relates stories about the many famous people and events associated with the inns. To name just a few, George Washington once drilled his troops on the lawn of the Beekman Arms in Rhinebeck, New York. Diamond Jim Brady, Lillian Russell, and hundreds of other celebrities once summered at the Adelphi Hotel in Saratoga Springs, New York. Ernest Hemingway used to break bread with one of his old European comrades at the Carriage House Inn in Searsport, Maine.

The photographs and text of *Historic Inns of the Northeast* can be used and enjoyed by readers on several levels—as an introduction to American history witnessed by these venerable lodgings, as an illustrated source of early architectural and interior design and an inspiration for decorating ideas, and as a practical travel guide with addresses and reservation phone numbers.

We encourage you to make these historic inns part of your personal history.

(Opposite) *The foyer in the Old Post House Inn.*

# Lincoln House Country Inn

## DENNYSVILLE, MAINE

FOR SEVERAL CENTURIES the climactic defeat of the British Gen. Charles, Lord Cornwallis at the Battle of Yorktown, Virginia, in 1787 and the Lincoln House were tied together in an unusual way.

Cornwallis' sword, which the general had surrendered to one of George Washington's aides, Gen. Benjamin Lincoln, had hung in the handsome Georgian colonial home in Dennysville, Maine, until it was moved to the permanent collection of the National Museum of American History, part of the Smithsonian Institution in Washington, D.C.

**BUILT IN 1791**

*The same year that the U.S. Congress passed the first internal revenue law, a tax on distilled spirits.*

The center-chimney house had been built by Theodore Lincoln, son of the general, using 15 skilled craftsmen from Massachusetts.

The Lincoln House had many other unusual brushes with history. For example, the famous naturalist-artist, J. J. Audubon, stayed there in 1834 on his way to an expedition in Labrador. As a thank you to his hosts for their elaborate hospitality, he named a new bird that he had discovered on his journey the "Lincoln Sparrow."

This historic house at the head of the Dennys River has now become the Lincoln House Country Inn, surrounded by 95 acres of woods and banks of day lilies and wild roses.

Furnishings in the inn have been described as eclectic antique and include reproduction Chippendale and Queen Anne chairs in the dining room, an old hand-painted dog sled, and a spectacular 1921 Steinway grand piano. The Woodshed Pub, part of the inn, boasts a 4,000-pound elm log bar.

If J. J. Audubon were alive today, he would still feel right at home in the surrounding woods. On a bird-watching expedition one July day several years ago, more than 100 different species were sighted.

*The all-brick fireplace displays an array of early cookingware. Note the pots on the iron arm, which was pushed back into the fireplace to heat soups and stews.*

(Opposite) *This handsome Georgian colonial was built by Theodore Lincoln, the son of Gen. Benjamin Lincoln who had accepted the sword of surrender from British general Lord Cornwallis at Yorktown.*

(Opposite, above left) *Some of the walls of the inn are covered with half-paneling. The Queen Anne-style chair pictured here reflects the curvilinear design that was popular among 18th- and early 19th-century furniture makers.*

(Opposite, above right) *Pictured here is one of the 17 guest rooms, where an iron woodburning stove brings a frontier touch to a hideaway stocked with books. There are no telephones or TVs in the guest rooms. Such modern amenities have been relegated to the inn's Woodshed Pub to preserve the guests' peaceful enjoyment of a quieter era.*

(Opposite, below) *In early evening, guests gather in this second floor conversation area to meet one another, enjoy the old prints on the wall, and await dinner, which is served promptly at 7 p.m.*

(Above) *Seen here is a portion of the Lincoln House parlor. The building's date of construction appears in gold letters on the black fire screen.*

(Right) *This close-up of the parlor fireplace shows the classic motifs on the mantel and the brass plate and bell antiques collected by the current owners.*

*Lincoln House Country Inn*
**Routes 1 and 86**
**Dennysville, ME 04628**
**Reservations: 207/726-3953**

4 guest rooms with private baths; 7 with semi-private baths. Dinner and a full country breakfast are included in the rates.

6

# *The Carriage House Inn*

## Searsport, Maine

On a summer evening several years ago a group of children gathered in a room of the Carriage House Inn in Searsport, Maine, suddenly became unusually quiet. According to the subsequent stories, they may have been visited by the dwelling's resident "spirit," Capt. John McGilvery.

Captain John, who was the builder of the house, was reportedly a friendly ghost. It seems, however, that he was a silent visitor, which was too bad. He certainly could have told some fascinating tales.

He could have described, for example, his days as a sea captain when Searsport, Maine, was one of the thriving early homes of the great American sailing ships. He could have told how he built his large Victorian home right across from Penobscot Bay. And he could have recounted stories of the mansion's interesting occupants down through the years, among whom he would surely have numbered the late Waldo Pierce, a noted Maine painter. Perhaps he would have even remembered an infrequent guest of Waldo's, a great storyteller who had served with the artist in the ambulance corps during World War I, Ernest Hemingway.

**BUILT IN 1874**

*The same year that an elephant was used for the first time to symbolize the Republican party. It appeared in a* Harper's Weekly *cartoon.*

The home became an inn during the 1980s, but Captain McGilvery's spirit would still have recognized many of the structure's original features, including the large rooms with high ceilings decorated with medallions and crown moldings. There are three handsome fireplaces on the first floor: a slate fireplace in the open kitchen and dining area, another in the den, and a third with a marble mantel in the formal living room.

Three guest rooms, located on the third floor, are furnished with 19th-century beds and chairs, and they all have fireplaces. An attached carriage house now serves as an antique shop, one of many scattered throughout Searsport.

With such a pleasant place in which to dwell, it is no wonder that the spirit of Captain McGilvery is so good-natured.

*A statue of a young boy waters a garden of perennials on the front lawn, shaded by white birch, elm, oak, and cedar trees.*

(Opposite) *Ernest Hemingway may have warmed himself by this parlor fireplace when he visited Waldo Pierce, the owner of the home in the 1950s. Pierce, a famed Maine painter, had served in the ambulance corps with Hemingway during World War I.*

(Above) *A white carousel horse, circa 1950, leads the way to the Carriage House, now an antique and art gallery.*

(Opposite, above left) *A golden statue of Julius Caesar obligingly points the way to the guest rooms as he stands on a landing of the stairway.*

(Opposite, below left) *A sitting area on the inn's second floor doubles as a library and offers a window view of Penobscot Bay.*

*The Carriage House Inn*

**Route One**

**Searsport, ME 04974**

**Reservations: 207/548-2289**

**5 guest rooms. A breakfast of fresh-baked rolls, coffee cake, and fresh fruit is included in the rates.**

(Above) *A large Oriental rug covers the dining room floor. Each morning this table is filled with freshly baked rolls, muffins, and coffee cake with individual cups of fresh fruit for each guest.*

# The Captain Lord Mansion

## KENNEBUNKPORT, MAINE

WERE IT NOT FOR THE OUTBREAK of the War of 1812, the Captain Lord Mansion might never have been built. For it was the British blockade during the conflict that idled many shipbuilders in Maine and gave rise to the mansion's birth.

**STARTED IN 1812**

*The same year that the United States declared war on Great Britain because of British seizures of American ships and seamen on the high seas.*

It took more than two years to construct the coastal structure that Nathaniel Lord, a merchant and shipbuilder, commissioned. Unfortunately he died at age 39, only a few months after he and his wife moved into their new home.

A succession of family members lived in the house, including Charles P. Clark, the president of the New York & New Haven Railroad, who had married one of the Lord family daughters. In 1898 he decided to remodel the house, top to bottom, adding a main center staircase, an 18-foot bay window to the dining area, and numerous Victorian touches.

The present-day owners, Bev Davis and her husband Rick Litchfield, have continued these romantic additions with even greater flair. Each of the guest rooms is named after one of Captain Lord's ships and is a picture of elegance. For example, the Brig Merchant room contains a high canopy bed made of Honduran mahogany, a huge armoire, an English dressing table, and plush red carpeting. On the third floor, the Ship Harvest room offers a fireplace, a four-poster bed with carved headboard, and a handsome mural scene of early Kennebunkport.

A highlight of a visit here is the breakfast of fresh-baked muffins, French vanilla yogurt, continental-style eggs, coffee, and herbal teas which is served family style in the country kitchen.

*The Captain Lord Mansion was built by ship carpenters idled by the War of 1812. Captain Lord had wisely kept his ships in port during the hostilities.*

*A well-travelled steamer trunk becomes a handsome plant stand in the inn's Ship Harvest Room. Each of the 16 guest chambers is named after a ship constructed by Nathaniel Lord, the original owner of the mansion.*

*The 18-foot bay windows in the parlor light a chess game on a Chippendale table and chairs.*

(Opposite) *Note the painstaking carved detail on each of the four bedposts in the Ship Calendar Room. A two-step ladder helps guests clamber into the high Sheraton bed.*

# The Captain Lord Mansion

**The Captain Lord Mansion**
**P.O. Box 800**
**Kennebunkport, ME 04046**
**Reservations: 207/967-3141**

16 guest rooms, each with private bath; 11 rooms have working fireplaces. A full breakfast is included in the rates.

(Right) *At the Captain Lord Mansion, a 19th-century bake oven in the parlor becomes the perfect place for making homemade bread or warming glogg.*

*An Oriental screen and rug add exotic touches to the more traditional furnishings of the parlor. Each afternoon guests are served refreshments here, iced tea on summer days and hot Swedish glogg (a cranapple and spice concoction) or a choice of 20 different teas in winter.*

# The Admiral's Quarters Inn

## BOOTHBAY HARBOR, MAINE

IN THE 17TH CENTURY a band of Indians gathered near beautiful Boothbay Harbor in Maine for a fateful bargaining session with the new white settlers. After an extensive debate, the Indians finally accepted 30 beaver pelts for the harbor, an arrangement that suggests they were either incredibly poor bargainers or just a passing tribe with no stake in the area anyway.

**BUILT IN 1830**

*The same year that the Mormon Church was founded at Fayette, New York.*

Boothbay quickly became a boat-building center and a haven for ships from all over the world. In 1830, one sea captain found an ideal spot for a home on a knoll overlooking the water. There he built a 16-room mansion for himself with a view of his ship.

Jean and George Duffy are now the owners/managers of the sea captain's home, which they have converted into an inn. They have furnished each of the guest rooms with colonial period pieces and queen-size beds, put down blue or rose wall-to-wall carpeting to contrast with the white walls, and stripped off the front porch, turning it into a wide harbor-view deck where a continental breakfast is served each morning. A lawn slopes from the white building right down to the ocean.

"Our guests love to spend time on the deck," says Jean Duffy. "Then many of them take harbor cruises and shop, shop, shop in the nearby antique stores. They also come to dine on wonderful lobster."

One of the highlights of breakfast on the deck is the daily greeting tour conducted by Finn, the innkeeper's wolfhound.

*This white frame inn with black shutters is located right on Boothbay Harbor. The long landscaped lawn seen in this photo slopes down to the water.*

*The Admiral's Quarters Inn*
**105 Commercial Street**
**Boothbay Harbor, ME 04538**
**Reservations: 207/633-2474**

10 guest rooms. A continental breakfast is included in the rates. Closed during the winter months.

(Left) *A white wicker chair and a colonial clothes tree are some of the simple furnishings of this loft guest room. The bold floral prints on the chair upholstery and bedspread introduce more contemporary notes.*

(Below) *Brass andirons and colonial cookingware add pleasing accents to this stark white-brick fireplace.*

*An antique wooden horse with a yellow tail perches whimsically, and precariously, on a windowsill.*

(Following pages) *From the inn's porch and many of the guest room windows, one can watch the daily bustle of boats in Boothbay Harbor. The harbor is a landlocked haven for vessels of all shapes and sizes and the site of several major regattas each summer.*

DOUBLE EAGLE
BOOTHBAY HARBOR, ME.

# The Squire Tarbox Inn

## Wiscasset, Maine

Innkeeper Bill Mitman thinks cows are "too big" and chickens are "dumb." He and his wife Karen wanted to raise "animals with some personality" at their country inn in the center of a Maine island.

They chose goats.

Bill and Karen gave up the high-pressure city life and prestigious jobs with a major hotel chain to run the Squire Tarbox Inn, complete with a barn full of gentle Nubian goats which they milk daily to create award-winning cheeses. Goat milk is used in the everyday operation of the inn, in the blueberry nut muffins, nut loaf, and pound cake. It is served on cereals in the morning and even converted to goat milk soap for the guests' bathrooms.

The original homestead was built in 1763. Some of the boards from this house were used in the new farmhouse that Squire Tarbox built on the site in 1825. "Squire" was an honorary title given to Tarbox by the townspeople in respect for his great wealth, no singular honor in an island that was once home to some of the wealthiest people in Maine. Fifty-four sailing vessels based here caught fresh fish for the Boston market.

**STARTED IN 1763**

*The same year that one of the English colonies in America was given a new name, Vermont (meaning "green mountain" in French).*

The inn is a rambling structure shaped like an L, with many of the original fireplaces and beams still in place. There are no tennis courts or swimming pools. Guests come here primarily to relax, to bird-watch in a nearby saltwater marsh, to walk through hills of wild flowers, and to see the daily goat-milking ceremony.

Mr. Mitman describes his business this way: "We have all the dimensions of a working farm and all the comforts of a well-respected full-service inn, with a country simplicity."

*Squire Tarbox's original barn is the centerpiece of the inn that bears his name. Part of a working 12-acre farm, the estate boasts a flock of purebred goats who are responsible for the wonderful farmstead chevre and tellicherry crottin (cheese rolled into cracked tellicherry pepper) that show up regularly on the inn's tables.*

(Opposite) *A 19th-century horsedrawn sled serves to welcome visitors to the inn. Nearby is a pine-needled path that leads to a saltwater inlet.*

The Squire Tarbox Inn
Welcome
DINNER by Reservation
GOAT CHEESE

BARNS

## *The Squire Tarbox Inn*

**RR 2, Box 620**
**Wiscasset, ME 04578**
**Reservations: 207/882-7693**

11 guest rooms are furnished with "up-country" furniture and a few antiques. Breakfast is included in the rates; dinner is available.

(Above, left) *A beautiful hanging quilt adds a striking touch to this guest room, with two kitten pillows providing a playful air.*

(Above) *The inn's parlor is reflected in this carved antique mirror.*

(Previous pages) *A host of lamps light the high-ceilinged barn now converted to a guest library and rustic retreat. Note the cast-iron woodburning stove and the antique collectibles, from a checkerboard to chinaware, that line one of the barn's original beams.*

# The Bradford Inn

## Bradford, New Hampshire

Throughout the second half of the 19th century, traveling salesmen and stagecoach passengers gathered at the friendly Bradford Hotel in Bradford, New Hampshire. The nearby West Branch River was the major draw; it could be forded easily at this spot by horses and coaches, and it powered many mills in the surrounding area.

A hotel replaced the original structure in 1898. At that time the local newspaper proclaimed, "The new building is now being constructed on the site of the old Bradford Hotel and we can be justly proud of it as it marks a new era of history in our town." It even had such novelties as electric lights, with carriages and horses especially for ladies, according to a hotel brochure.

The three-story hotel has mellowed with time, losing some of its commercial veneer and becoming a more relaxed place to stay. But the Bradford Inn, now owned and managed by Tom and Connie Mazol, still retains many trappings of its earlier hotel days.

**BUILT IN 1898**

*The same year that the battleship Maine was blown up in the Havana harbor, sparking the Spanish–American War.*

"The Bradford Inn is one of the few remaining country inns that opened its doors as true inns," says Mr. Mazol. "It is not a mansion conversion or a large family home but a country hotel with wide halls, a grand staircase, and cheerful rooms." Many of the guest room furnishings date back to the turn of the century, and unusual items abound in the public areas, including needlework prints from the late 19th century, early photographs of a local family, and a still-functioning push pedal Singer sewing machine. Two large parlors downstairs are furnished with country and antique tables and chairs with a Victorian ambience.

Meals are served in the J. Albert Restaurant on the first floor and may range from J. Albert's Veal (a cutlet in a brandy cream sauce with apples and spices) to Molly Stark's Chicken (a boneless breast with sauteed onion and a sour cream sauce).

About all that's really missing from the early days are the "carriages and horses especially for ladies."

*Bright pink napkins and white tablecloths welcome guests to a dinner strongly influenced by the* Fanny Farmer Cookbook, *which was much in vogue at the turn of the century. The inn's specialties, adapted from Fanny's famous recipes, include veal and duck dishes.*

*Many of the furnishings in this parlor date back to 1898, the year of the inn's debut.*

(Above) *Located near a ford of the West Branch River, the Bradford Inn became a popular stopping point for 19th- and early-20th-century salesmen as they headed for the mills that lined the river's banks.*

(Right) *A white swan planter box graces a streetside garden filled with rose bushes. A copse of maples and pines grows between the inn and the West Branch River.*

*The Bradford Inn*
**RFD 1, Box 40**
**Main Street**
**Bradford, NH 03221**
**Reservations: 603/938-5309**

**12 guest rooms (including 6 that are two-room suites). A full breakfast is included in the rates.**

# White Goose Inn

## Orford, New Hampshire

In the mid-18th century settlers along the upper Connecticut River were alarmed by a rash of Indian raids. To help prevent these attacks, they established "fort towns" along the river.

Orford, New Hampshire, was one of these towns. Thomas Sawyer and his two eldest sons, attracted by the new security in the area, built a small white house here.

The home became a "work in progress" over succeeding decades as countless owners left their own personal marks on the structure. In 1833, for example, a successful local tanner by the name of Cutter added a brick wing. Twenty years later another owner, Elliot P. Johnson, fronted the building with a "Colonial Revival" porch.

**STARTED IN 1766**

*The same year that the Stamp Act (the British law that placed a tax on numerous types of goods imported into America which infuriated many of the colonists) was repealed by the English Parliament.*

The continuously enlarged home has gradually been remodelled to include all the necessities of modern living, except for telephones and television sets. The present owners, Mondred and Karin Wolf, have refused to introduce these somewhat jarring devices into guest rooms that are furnished with authentic colonial period pieces.

Guests can spend a quiet day enjoying the inn's eight acres (including a pond) or visit nearby Hanover, home of Dartmouth College.

And at night they can return to the comfortable cumulative handiwork of the Sawyer, Cutter, Johnson, and Wolf families—now named the White Goose Inn.

*While the inn has been completely renovated, a lantern and wall stencil are remnants of the building's early history.*

(Opposite) *This red brick building was an 1833 addition to a smaller wood framed house started before the American Revolutionary War by Thomas Sawyer, one of the first settlers of Orford, New Hampshire.*

(Above) *Pictured here is a split-level guest room, with a four-poster bed on the lower level and stairs leading to a sitting area.*

*White Goose Inn*
**Route 10**
**P. O. Box 17**
**Orford, NH 03777**
**Reservations: 603/353-4812**

**15 guest rooms. A continental breakfast (often featuring "baby" pancakes) is included in the rates.**

*Baby pancakes, the morning specialty of the inn, are served in this green-and-white dining room. Breakfast is the only meal the inn prepares, but the hosts refer guests to their favorite nearby restaurants for lunch and dinner.*

(Opposite, below) *Thomas Sawyer and his family would probably feel right at home in the White Goose's parlor today. Note the leaf pattern stenciled on the floor. It is a variation of the border running along the upper edges of the walls.*

# Juniper Hill Inn

## WINDSOR, VERMONT

DID YOU KNOW that Vermont was once a separate country, with its own constitution and currency? It was formed in 1777 when portions of New York and New Hampshire broke away from their parent states and created their own constitution at a tavern in Windsor, Vermont. Four years later this tiny independent nation entered the United States as the 14th state.

**BUILT IN 1902**

*The same year that the first Rose Bowl football game was played in Pasadena, California.*

The historic signing of the Vermont constitution took place just a mile from the present site of the Juniper Hill Inn.

The building was constructed atop Juniper Hill for Maxwell Evarts, a successful New York attorney, and it remained in his family until 1944. Then it became, successively, an inn, a nursing home, and a Catholic retreat center.

In 1984, Jim and Krisha Pennino purchased the retreat and began to slowly return the building to its earlier incarnation as an inn.

As guests drive up the hill, they are greeted by a panoramic view of the New Hampshire and Vermont countryside. This is followed by another impressive sight, that of the inn's Ionic portico, which is shaped like a miniature temple. Entering the inn, guests find themselves in a greatroom with a ceiling that is 10 feet high. Many pause in front of the room's huge central fireplace with its floor-to-ceiling chimney. Dominating the space is a massive oak library table, measuring 5 feet by 15 feet and weighing approximately 1,000 pounds.

The guest rooms are furnished with a mixture of antiques gathered by the innkeepers on their travels through the United States and Europe. Some of the chairs, which date to the Victorian age, have been reupholstered for comfort.

*A table full of current magazines, shelves full of books, and built-in seating on both sides of the fireplace are open invitations to a long, leisurely read on a sleepy afternoon. The hanging antique cookware harkens back to the days when families cooked their meals over the open flames of a fireplace.*

(Opposite) *Guests in the dining room pictured here might feast on such specialties as roast Cornish hen with raspberry sauce and stuffed breast of veal.*

(Opposite, above) *The stark white front of this Greek Revival–style building gives only a hint of the inn's overall size, concealing two wings of guest rooms. Juniper Hill has a total of 28 public rooms and guest chambers.*

(Opposite, below left) *The inn's perennial gardens bloom from early spring to late October with platoons of daises in June followed by a host of phlox in July and August and a whole army of wide black-eyed Susans in September.*

(Opposite, below right) *Theodore Roosevelt might well have sat on this carved, antique rocker during his 1903 visit to the inn.*

(Below) *The floral green drapes and spread add a regal touch to the queen-size bed in this guest room while a decanter of sherry with two glasses welcomes a couple to a romantic weekend.*

*Juniper Hill Inn*
**RR 1, Box 79**
**Windsor, VT 05089**
**Reservations: 802/674-5273**

**15 guest rooms with private baths; 9 of these rooms have working fireplaces. Breakfast (featuring eggs, whole wheat toast, French toast, and apple or peach pancakes served with homemade preserves) is included in the rates.**

# The Echo Lake Inn

## LUDLOW, VERMONT

"HE SAID HE WAS AGAINST IT." That's how President Calvin Coolidge described a minister's long sermon about sin.

One wonders how this man of few words might have described his frequent visits to Echo Lake Inn, near his home in Plymouth, Vermont.

Perhaps he would have said, "Wonderful location." It is, after all, right on Echo Lake in the Green Mountains.

"Impressive" is a word that might have come to him. The white and green building is four stories high with a porch running across the entire front, dotted by red rockers.

However Coolidge might have described the inn in his day, there is no denying the mouth-watering culinary delights offered by the current owners, Phil and Kathy Cocco. Highlights of the menu are zucchini stuffed with goat's cheese, scallions, and bacon and the veal escallops sauteed with shallots and chives.

**BUILT IN 1840**

*The same year that the Olympic Theater opened in New York City. Tickets were 25¢ each.*

When the Coccos bought the inn, they redecorated every room with new wallpaper and paintings, and they refinished all of the furniture. They also added such novel touches as the Stoned Tavern in the basement (named after the exposed foundation walls) and on the first floor the Basket Case Lounge, featuring Kathy's collection of antique baskets.

The inn is located in the tiny community of Tyson just outside of Ludlow. A general store and the Tyson Congregational Church—built in 1894—are about the only other large structures for miles around.

"Don't need much more," said a local resident laconically.

Perhaps he was one of Calvin's relatives.

*In a guest bathroom, lace coverall and hand-embroidered towels provide delicate contrasts to the rough warp and woof of a country rocking chair.*

(Opposite) *The lounge ceiling is a riot of baskets of different sizes, shapes, and textures. Note the photograph on the wall at left. That is "Silent" Calvin Coolidge, 28th president of the United States and a frequent inn visitor.*

Vermont Life

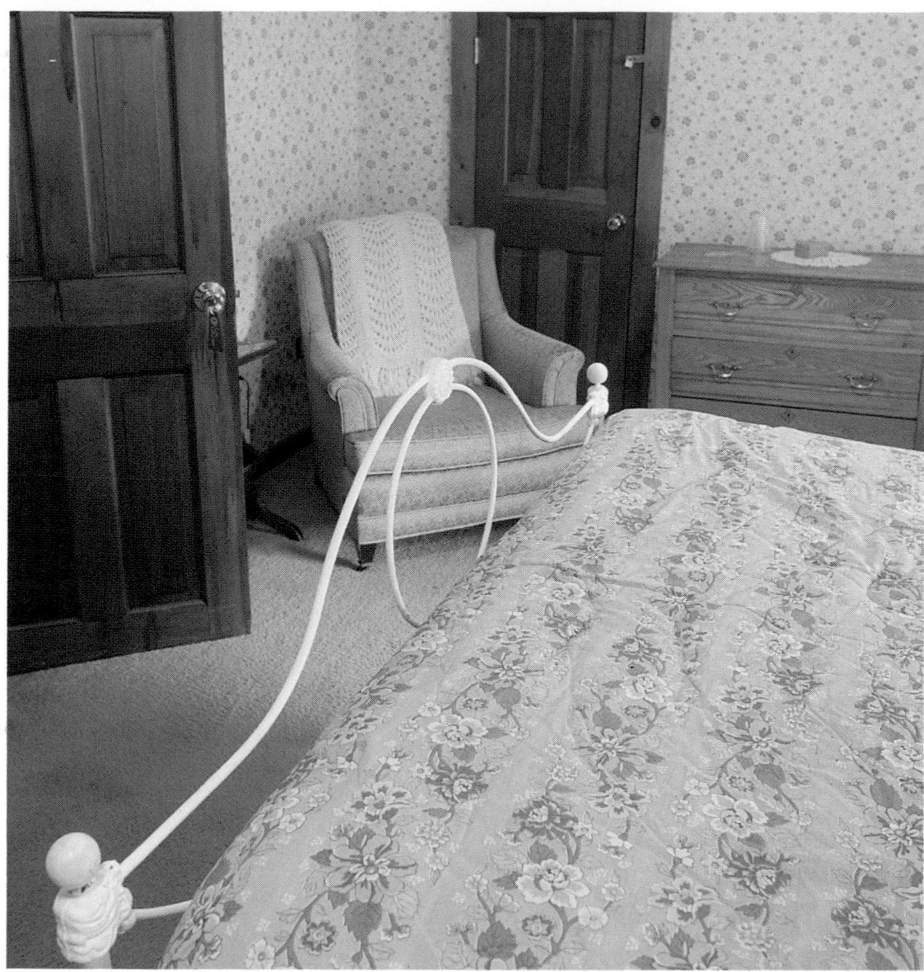

(Above, left) *Pictured here is the Tyson Room, a guest chamber named after the tiny town in which the Echo Lake Inn is situated.*

(Above, right) *The painting in the parlor seen here is a reminder of the inn's location, only minutes away from two major Vermont ski areas, Killington and Okemo.*

(Right) *An aging duck decoy, three books, an old cigar box, a basket, and a "6-1/2" wooden shoe create an eclectic still-life decoration in the dining room.*

(Opposite) *Wide, comfortable, antique maple furnishings fill the parlor, forming several inviting conversational groupings.*

*The Echo Lake Inn*
**Box 154**
**Ludlow, VT 05149**
**Reservations: 802/228-8602**

**28 guest rooms and 6 condominiums. Breakfast, lunch (weekends only), and dinner are served.**

(Right) *Echo Lake's white frame building stands four stories high with a front porch stretching 60 feet across. The cost of construction was considered high in 1840, an outrageous $3,500.*

(Below) *A white wicker chair and a red rocker are handsome porchmates. The inn's long porch is an ideal place to catch a breeze in this Vermont Lake Region.*

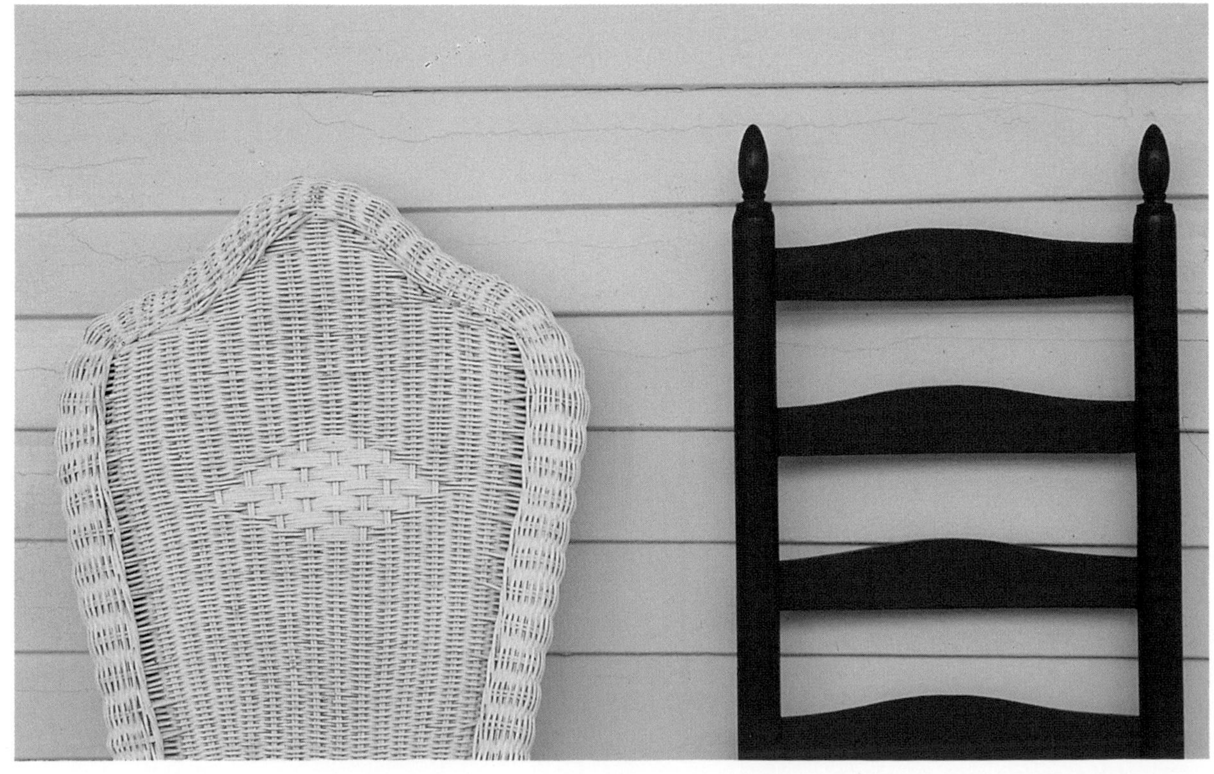

# *Vermont Marble Inn*

## Fair Haven, Vermont

In the 1860s golden marble blocks were cut from a quarry in West Haven, Vermont. As in the days of the Egyptian pyramids, each block was numbered. The marble was then hauled by oxen to a site on the Village Green in Fair Haven.

**BUILT IN 1867**

*The same year that the United States purchased Alaska from Russia.*

Ira C. Allen, a descendant of Vermont's famous Ethan Allen, was using the marble to build his masterpiece, a home for himself and his family. Some say that he was motivated by the desire to display the wealth that he had earned in the marble business. Others said he was trying to outshine a former partner who was building a house on the other side of the Green.

Whatever Mr. Allen's motives, the results were undeniably splendid—an Italianate Victorian home filled with seven chandeliers, carved marble fireplaces, and countless plaster wall decorations.

This marble palace was turned into an inn by three former New Yorkers, Bea and Richard Taube and Shirley Stein. They have kept much of Mr. Allen's original vision but have added their own touches everywhere. Each of the guest rooms—which are named for famous romantic poets—lives up to its name by featuring such quaint, intimate touches as a four-poster bed and lace curtains. Some of the rooms even have fireplaces.

Dinners are served in a formal dining room under a ceiling of papier mâché and plaster designs. The award-winning cuisine includes breast of chicken sauteed with leeks, tomatoes, and roasted peppers and grilled rack of lamb with pommery mustard and herbs.

*This Italianate mansion, which stands squarely on the Village Green, was built from local marble quarried by the descendants of Revolutionary War hero Ethan Allen.*

## Vermont Marble Inn

(Right) *The William Shakespeare Room has a proper English air with a Victorian settee and a canopy bed for midsummer night dreams.*

(Right) *The builders of what had once been the home of Ira C. Allen and family certainly did not stint on marble. In addition to the fireplace seen on page 49, the parlor pictured here contains another masterpiece, a fireplace with a plethora of hand-carved shapes and symbols.*

(Below) *Guests are surrounded by marble even as they sit on white wicker chairs on the porch.*

*Vermont Marble Inn*
12 West Park Place
Fair Haven, VT 05743
Reservations: 802/265-8383

12 guest rooms. A complimentary breakfast is included in the rates.

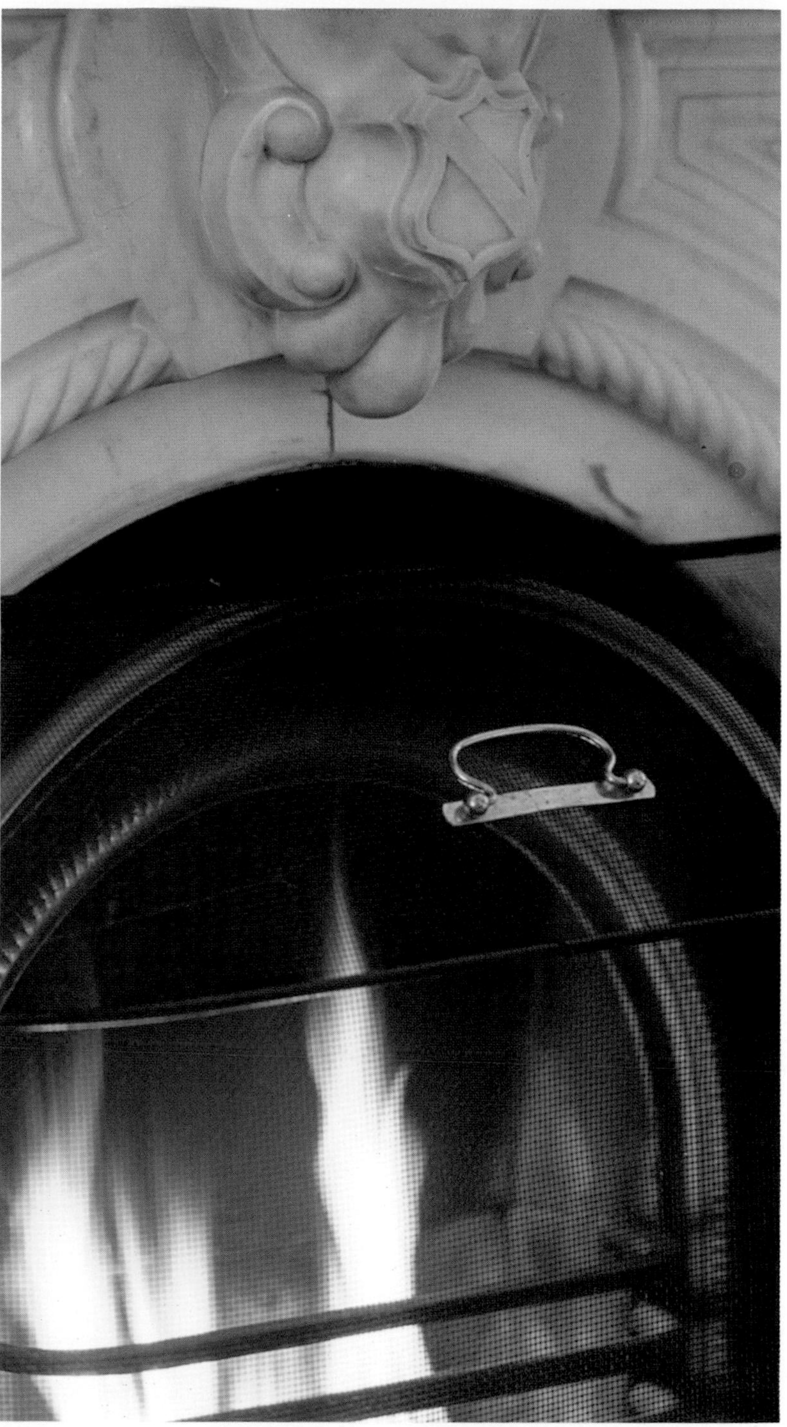

(Above) *"Give me the luxuries, and anyone can have the necessaries," wrote Oscar Wilde, who would certainly have appreciated the extravagantly carved marble fireplace in the room named for him at the Vermont Marble Inn. All of the inn's other guest rooms take the names of famous authors as well.*

# The Inn on Cove Hill

## Rockport, Massachusetts

The seacoast around Rockport, Massachusetts, is lined with jagged rocks and coves, attracting whale-watchers and artists alike. In the 18th century the rugged terrain also offered numerous hiding places for the loot that pirates stole from passing ships. Sometime in the 1790s Joshua Norwood stumbled across one of these caches at Gully Point.

**BUILT IN 1791**

*The same year that chief executive George Washington initiated the custom of holding a public reception at the President's Mansion on New Year's Day.*

Norwood used this unexpected gold to build a new house for his son. And this Federal-style house with a view of the harbor and ocean soon showed what a pirate's booty could buy. Wide pumpkin-pine floorboards were used throughout the structure, complementing wood-paneled walls and crown and dental moldings.

This 13-room castle remained in the Norwood family until the mid-1950s when it was sold and began a second life as an inn. Marjorie and John Pratt purchased it in 1979 and undertook a careful restoration. Each of the guest rooms is furnished with antique and reproduction pieces reflecting the early days of the Norwood family and all of the rooms are decorated with country-style fabrics and wallpaper. At night guests can sleep much as the Norwoods did, in four-poster canopy beds or in the later Victorian brass-and-iron versions.

Freshly baked pumpkin muffins are available for breakfast along with juice and coffee or tea. Breakfast is usually served in the garden in the front of the house, but on cold or chilly days it is brought to each guest's room on an individual tray.

After breakfast guests often go shopping for art and antiques in Rockport. A few might even poke around Gully's Point to see what turns up.

*This is the scene from one of the inn's three balconies. Summer brings a high tide of fishing enthusiasts and artists to this Rockport waterfront.*

(Opposite) *The guest rooms at the Inn on Cove Hill are furnished with country-style beds and fabrics and 19th-century armoires, on floors of wide pumpkin-pine boards.*

# The Inn on Cove Hill

(Left) *This Federal-style building, which was home to the Norwood family for more than 200 years, was reportedly built with pirates' booty discovered in a nearby cove.*

(Below) *Although all 11 of the inn's guest rooms have private or shared baths, the country washstand with pitcher and bowl seen here are reminders of the days before indoor plumbing.*

*The Inn on Cove Hill*
**37 Mount Pleasant Street**
**Rockport, MA 01966**
**Reservations: 508/546-2701**

**11 guest rooms. A continental breakfast is included in the rates.**

# The Old Yarmouth Inn

## YARMOUTH PORT, MASSACHUSETTS

WHEN THE LAST NAIL was driven into place in 1696, the Wayside Staging Inn became an official stagecoach stop on Cape Cod. According to research by the present owners, that founding year makes the inn (later renamed Old Yarmouth Inn) the oldest on the historic cape.

**BUILT IN 1694–1696**

*The same period that King William's War erupted in America (later known as the first French and Indian War).*

During its long history of hospitality, the inn has listened to the reverberating tones of orator Daniel Webster and given shelter to writer and nature enthusiast Henry David Thoreau. In more recent times guests have included Judy Garland and numerous political figures.

Located on two acres, the 10-room inn is framed by tall oak and maple trees and ringed by flowering bulbs, roses, and wildflowers. Inside, the colonial theme reflects the inn's early days. It is expressed in period antiques in all of the public and guest rooms.

A full breakfast is served, and all other meals are available. One of the specialties of the house, the pride of the chef, is seafood chowder which is arguably the "best on Cape Cod." At dinner entrées include grilled New England swordfish served with a lemon butter sauce, Seafood Imperial (a casserole of lobster, shrimp, and scallops topped with a lobster sauce), and grilled rack of lamb served on a Dijon mustard rosemary demi-glace.

A live classical jazz group plays most nights in the inn's Stagecoach Lounge. Perhaps an earlier age saw Daniel Webster and Henry David Thoreau tapping their boots on the inn's wooden planks in time with musicians of their day.

*A half-buried iron anchor is a fitting symbol of Cape Cod's seafaring past and of the island's oldest inn.*

*Double time. Twin antique clocks summon guests to breakfast in the dining room.*

*With their nautical prints and colonial furnishings, the guest chambers of the Old Yarmouth Inn would have made sea captains of the 19th century feel welcome. These old salts would also have approved of the rooms' names—Barnstable Harbor, Chatham Harbor, Quisset Harbor, Rock Harbor, and Wellfeet Harbor.*

*The Old Yarmouth Inn*

**233 Main Street (Route 6A)**
**Yarmouth Port, MA 02675**
**Reservations 508/362-3191**

**5 guest rooms. A full breakfast is included in the rates.**

*The wallpaper pattern on the front stairway proudly boasts an American eagle and the motto stamped on many U.S. coins—"E pluribus unum," meaning "out of many, one."*

*Seen here is one of two fireplaces in the "Publick Room." The Chinese vases on the mantel are subtle reminders of the age when the China trade was a vital part of Nantucket's economy. The grand piano is for guests who like to mix a little Beethoven with their leisure.*

# The Four Chimneys

## NANTUCKET, MASSACHUSETTS

NANTUCKET IS ONLY 49 SQUARE MILES, but this tiny island occupies a commanding presence just south of Cape Cod. Indeed, its location made it a magnet for the great whaling and cargo sailing ships of the 17th and 18th centuries.

Orange Street on Nantucket exerted a similar pull on ships' captains, some 126 of whom built their homes along its tree-lined way. Among these seamen was Capt. Frederick Gardner, who constructed a 22-room mansion on Orange Street in 1835.

Some 20 years later Mr. Freeman Adams saw this large home and decided that it had financial possibilities as an inn for sailors and early travelers to the island. So he purchased the captain's home, christened it the "Bay View House," and placed advertisements for his new lodging place in the local paper, promising that "no pains will be spared to insure the comfort of its patrons."

**BUILT IN 1835**

*The same year that the Liberty Bell in Philadelphia cracked while tolling for the death of Chief Justice John Marshall.*

The inn continues to live on, with yet another name, the Four Chimneys (named for the pair of chimneys on each side of the building).

Inside, five original "master rooms" await guests. Each is an oversized chamber with a fireplace, canopy bed, and Oriental rugs. Smaller rooms are available on several of the floors. A suite on the third floor has wonderful harbor views.

Guests can relax in a double parlor with twin fireplaces on the first floor. This room is furnished with Chinese rugs and Oriental antiques, elegant cargo from the 18th-century sea trade that once flourished between the United States and China.

After a continental breakfast, served either in guest rooms or on the porch, visitors can explore the other sea captains' homes that still grace Orange Street.

*The Four Chimneys' bright red doorway sports an antique knocker and hardware. This mansion at 38 Orange Street was built by a sea captain, as were 126 other homes along the same thoroughfare.*

(Following pages) *A suite on the third floor has its own private balcony with harbor views.*

*The impressive inlaid dresser pictured here is a Dutch Marquetry Bombe mirrored commode.*

(Above) *Comfortable re-upholstered antiques and reproduction pieces encourage guests of the inn to linger for conversation in the parlor after a day of beach-bathing, sailing, or biking around town.*

(Below) *This brass, winged figure watches over an Empire period settee in the Patterson Guest Room.*

*The Four Chimneys*
**38 Orange Street**
**Nantucket, MA 02554**
**Reservations: 508/228-1912**

**A continental breakfast is included in the rates.**

# *Jared Coffin House*

## NANTUCKET, MASSACHUSETTS

THE JARED COFFIN HOUSE has become one of the most famous inns in New England, with its numerous attractions limned in countless guidebooks.

Mr. Jared Coffin himself would undoubtedly be quite pleased at the fame of the inn bearing his name. In the mid-19th century he prospered as an oil merchant and wanted to build a house that reflected his success. He selected plans for an imposing Greek Revival brick mansion that would be the first three-story building on the island of Nantucket.

Coffin enjoyed his new showplace for barely two years before moving to Boston. Then the Nantucket Steamboat Company purchased the house and turned it into a hotel. The Coffin House was later sold to the Nantucket Historical Trust, an organization that bought several nearby buildings to create an historic inn complex with 58 guest rooms.

**STARTED IN 1845**

*The same year that the Republic of Texas was annexed by the United States.*

Each guest room features a decorative period theme and includes a four-poster bed and private bath. Guests may sweep down the curved staircase to Jared's Restaurant, where harp or piano entertainment enhances the dining experience. Another alternative is the more informal Tap Room, where outdoor dining is available in warmer months. One of the favorite after-dinner treats is to simply go walking outside along Nantucket's cobblestone streets.

If Mr. Coffin was like modern visitors, he must have regretted leaving this beautiful place after so short a stay.

*Shining brass andirons in a lobby fireplace welcome guests to the high style that Jared Coffin brought to his home in the 1840s as he tried to outdo the other wealthy oil merchants in Nantucket.*

*A white sweeping staircase is highlighted by plush red carpeting and Japanese prints. The original owner, Jared Coffin, enjoyed all this beauty for only two years, after which he sold his home and returned to Boston.*

(Opposite) *This loft room with its canopy bed and other colonial furnishings is on the third floor, once a unique distinction. At the time of its construction, the house was the only three-story building in town.*

JARED COFFIN HOUSE

*Jared Coffin House*

**29 Broad Street**

**Nantucket, MA 02554**

**Reservations: 508/228-2400**

**58 guest rooms with twin or double beds. Breakfast is not included in the rates but all meals are available at the inn.**

(Opposite) *This Greek Revival building is in the heart of Nantucket's historic district, close to Steamboat Wharf.*

*Jared's Restaurant—great for fresh fish—is part of an addition that was made to the house in 1857, when it was converted from a private home to a hotel. The large oil painting along the right wall shows the Coffin children.*

# The Charlotte Inn

## Edgartown, Massachusetts

There's something about the Charlotte Inn that sends many writers into fits of verbal ecstasy.

"One of New England's most stylish little lodging enclaves," wrote Andrew Harper in his *Hideaway Report,* combining "the virtues of an art gallery, gourmet restaurant and country inn all in one."

**BUILT IN 1860**

*The same year that South Carolina became the first Southern state to secede from the Union.*

The *American Express Platinum Card* newsletter reported, "For the Conovers (innkeepers Gary and Paula), the Charlotte Inn is not just a business. It is a work of art that combines their love of antiques with the satisfaction of sharing their remarkable home with grateful guests."

Veteran inn book author Norman Simpson stayed there and thought that his accommodations had perhaps been "the ultimate country inn bedroom."

The subject of all this high praise was originally a sea captain's home in a neighborhood of Greek Revival houses in the slumbering Massachusetts community of Edgartown. Starting with this house, the Conovers have created an inn complex that includes guest rooms in an adjacent carriage house, a coach house, and two other nearby residences.

Each of the guest rooms has been decorated with extraordinary care, some displaying Ralph Lauren wallpaper, original paintings, and museum-quality objets d'art, as well as fireplaces and wall-to-wall carpeting. There are fresh flowers in the rooms and down pillows and comforters on the beds.

Guests can visit an art gallery on the first floor of the main house and dine at a French-style restaurant serving such specialties as ravioli of foie gras, leeks with a truffle and cognac cream sauce, and grilled rack and leg of lamb with goat cheese and cilantro sauce.

Small wonder that the Charlotte Inn has attracted so many enthusiastic press notices.

*A pretty basket of gardenias welcomes guests to the inn's brick-paved courtyard.*

*The main building of the inn, a three-story clapboard structure, was once a sea captain's house. Today it includes guest accommodations, a well-regarded restaurant, and an antique gallery.*

(Following pages) *The inn offers visitors a choice of al fresco dining in the garden or an indoor eatery with fresh-cut flowers on the table, hanging plants, and greenery on the stairs.*

*Horses in a variety of shapes and guises enliven the parlor, from the sculpture in the far left to the oil portrait over the door. Meanwhile, a decanter of sherry sits invitingly on the mantel of the white-wood-and-black-marble fireplace.*

*A silver brush, comb, and handmirror and turn-of-the-century cosmetic containers are beautifully showcased on a highly polished cherrywood dresser in one of the guest rooms.*

The Charlotte Inn

**South Summer Street**
**Edgartown, MA 02539**
**Reservations: 508/627-4751**

25 guest rooms in five separate buildings. A continental breakfast is included in the rates.

# The Daggett House

## EDGARTOWN, MASSACHUSETTS

THE DAGGETT HOUSE in Edgartown on Martha's Vineyard has an unusual secret. A secret staircase.

An ordinary bookcase in the wall swings open to reveal a landing that leads to a beautiful room. Newlyweds are fond of popping out of this staircase to surprise guests attending their reception. The staircase itself is lined with bottles signed by couples who have followed this tradition.

**STARTED IN 1660**

*The same year that the first divorce was granted in the colony of Delaware.*

The staircase has also been known to open and close on its own, pushed by a spirit on these occasions . . . or so they say. Perhaps the mischief-maker is even the ghost of John Daggett, who built a small tavern on this site in 1660. The public room of this tavern later became the breakfast room of the Daggett House when it was constructed in 1750. A portion of the breakfast room contains a "beehive" fireplace, so named because of its shape. And yes, a ghost has been reported here too. It has even been *photographed!* A picture owned by the current innkeepers shows a vague visage appearing just to the left of the fireplace.

Over the years the Daggett House has seen many owners and many changes. Initially it served as a sailors' boardinghouse. It then became a countinghouse during the 19th century when the whaling industry boomed. The home was purchased by Fred and Lucille Chirgwin in 1948 and converted to a bed & breakfast inn. The inn, now managed by two of the Chirgwin's sons, has become a resort complex comprised of the Daggett House and two neighboring buildings, the Captain Warren House and the Garden Cottage.

The owners make two suggestions to incoming guests. If you plan to arrive during the summer season, *always* make reservations for the ferry from the mainland.

And don't lean too hard against a bookcase in the dining room.

*Pictured here is the Daggett House's breakfast room, originally the public room of the first tavern licensed to serve beer on Martha's Vineyard.*

(Following pages) *Over the years, this entranceway has been used by customers when the building was a store, by captains of whalers when it was a countinghouse, and still later by sailors coming home to a boardinghouse.*

59

This photo provides a bird's-eye view of the Daggett House as seen from across the street. Many of the inn's windows have harbor views and the backyard slopes down to a small beach and dock.

In this guest room wooden bedposts and a lacy canopy frame a fireplace that predates the American Revolution.

*The Daggett House*

**59 North Water Street**

**Edgartown, MA 02539**

**Reservations: 508/627-4600**

18 guest rooms and 6 suites in three buildings. A continental breakfast is included in the rates.

*Look again! The bookcase swings open to reveal a hidden staircase. In what has become an inn tradition, newlyweds frequently burst from this hideaway to surprise wedding breakfast guests. The bottles glimpsed through the opening have been signed by couples following this tradition.*

*Look closely at this bookcase that was constructed as part of the original house. It contains a secret.*

# The Turning Point Inn

## Great Barrington, Massachusetts

The Turning Point Inn has three original Rumford fireplaces, all dating back to the early 19th century and all in working order. An inscription scrawled on the wall above one of them offers an interesting historic footnote. It reads, "Pixley 1843."

One of the original owners had apparently added this personal touch. In the mid-1700s, the king of England had awarded the Pixley family some choice New England land. The family built the Pixley Tavern on the site and it quickly became a stagecoach stop on the route between Boston and New York.

The inn, now named the Turning Point, retains much of its original structure, including the high ceilings and the wide-plank floors. When some 2-inch slabs of chestnut were found in walls being torn down, the new innkeepers turned them into large trestle tables. The guest rooms are furnished with colonial period pieces.

**BUILT IN 1802**

*The same year that the U.S. Military Academy opened at West Point, New York.*

Located on 11 acres of land, the inn is surrounded by large sugar maples and evergreen trees and flower beds.

One of the prime summer attractions is the world famous Tanglewood, summer home of the Boston Symphony, just 15 minutes away. The Norman Rockwell Museum and the Sterling and Francine Clark Art Institute are also nearby.

The innkeepers, Shirley and Jamie Yost, offer nutritional vegetarian breakfasts. A typical meal might include baked fruit, many-grain hot and cold cereals, and special pancakes.

*This part-brick, part-frame inn was built on the site of an 18th-century stagecoach stop between New York and Boston. Today it is only 15 minutes away from the Berkshire's famous Tanglewood Music Festival, featuring summer concerts by the Boston Symphony Orchestra.*

*Eggs and whole-grain pancakes are typical morning fare at the Turning Point. The trestle table, which is 2 inches thick, was crafted from 200-year-old chestnut wood discovered in the inn's original walls during the structure's restoration.*

The Turning Point Inn
RD 2
Box 140
Great Barrington, MA 01230
Reservations: 413/528-4777

9 guest rooms. A nutritional breakfast is included in the rates.

*The Turning Point's summer garden is a feast of flowers and colors, shaded by sugar maples. Nature walks and cross-country trails lace the inn's 11 acres.*

*In one of the guest quarters, which are simply but colorfully furnished, a handmade quilt becomes the perfect country compliment to the lathe-turned bed.*

*You can almost hear the clump of a stagecoach driver's boots on the original stairs and wide-plank floors pictured here.*

# Nathaniel Porter Inn

## Warren, Rhode Island

By 1981, it was hard to see the Federal period architecture—or anything else of value—in the multifamily tenement on Water Street in Warren, Rhode Island. Indeed, the old relic was scheduled for demolition.

But, at virtually the last minute, the building was saved by the Lynch family and carefully restored to its 18th-century appearance. Then it had been the home of a sea captain and Warren a hub of the nation's flourishing sea trade with the Orient, Europe, and the Mediterranean.

Today the sea captain's home is an inn, drawing its name from the owner's ancestor, Nathaniel Porter, who at the age of 13 fought in the Battle of Lexington.

Well-known for its cuisine, which the inn calls "international," the Nathaniel Porter was designated "one of America's finest restaurants" two years in a row by the Master Chefs of America. According to Robert Lynch, no other Rhode Island restaurant has ever achieved this distinction.

**BUILT IN 1795**

*The same year that the U.S. Congress, then sitting in New York, created the Post Office Department.*

Guests who come to sample this celebrated cuisine have their choice of five separate dining areas, each extensively furnished with antiques and works of art. They range from the formal—with wing-back chairs and candlelight—to an informal tavern room and a courtyard.

Like the public rooms, the guest rooms have been restored and furnished with antiques, including, in two of the three cases, canopied four-poster beds. They all have fireplaces and private bathrooms.

Guests looking for a bit of mayhem with their meal may be interested in the inn's Murder Mystery Dinners. Held the last Friday of every month, these evenings feature professional actors in an original play that moves from room to room.

*Guests of the Nathaniel Porter Inn have a choice of five dining areas. The Nathaniel Porter was designated "one of America's finest restaurants" two years in a row by the Master Chefs of America.*

*In 1981, this beautiful Federal-style building came within a hairsbreadth of the wrecking ball, but it was saved and restored by its present owners.*

**Nathaniel Porter Inn**
**125 Water Street**
**Warren, RI 02885**
**Reservations: 401/245-6622**

**3 guest rooms. A continental breakfast is included in the rates.**

(Far left) *This iron anchor in the garden is a rusty reminder of the building's first owner, a wealthy Rhode Island sea captain.*

(Left) *The mural in the dining room, depicting ancient ruins, was handpainted on large sections of paper and applied to the wall about 1810.*

*Each of the inn's three guest rooms offers lovers an ideal romantic hideaway. The cozy fireplace seen here is one of nine in the building. Four are kept burning throughout the winter months.*

# Old Lyme Inn

## OLD LYME, CONNECTICUT

OLD LYME was settled in 1665, close to the bend where the Connecticut River courses into the Long Island Sound. It was a location that prompted sea captains to purchase virtually every house in town.

**BUILT IN THE EARLY 1850s**

*The same period as that in which the California Gold Rush erupted at the opposite end of the continent.*

A notable exception was a rambling home built in the 1850s by the Champlains, a family of farmers, who lived on 300 acres of rich, black soil. A few years later, when weekend painters discovered the beauties of the local rural landscapes, the once isolated farmhouse suddenly found itself surrounded by artists daubing at easels. One of America's most celebrated early art colonies, the Old Lyme School of Art, moved into a Georgian mansion right across the road from the Champlain home. Artists such as Willard Metcalf, Childe Hassam, and Carleton Wiggs joined the colony and over the years their Impressionist paintings of the area have become quite valuable.

The Champlains sold their home in the early 1950s. The new owner turned it into a riding academy, where Jacqueline Bouvier (later to take the famous names of "Kennedy" and "Onassis") had her first riding lessons. Then it became a boarding house, the Barbizon Oaks, until it was almost destroyed by fire. Diana Field Atwood purchased the charred shell in 1976.

Atwood rebuilt and refurbished everything, thanks to a Midas touch in acquiring antiques—a Victorian bar from the oldest tavern in Pittsburgh (complete with tiny holes inflicted perhaps by tipsy dart throwers); a huge beveled mirror, purchased at auction for $5; and marble mantels from Connecticut mansions.

Guest and public rooms have been furnished with Victorian and Empire pieces and the walls adorned with paintings from the Old Lyme Art Colony. Some of the stenciling and wall murals offer excellent examples of the mid-1800s style of decorative arts once executed in local homes by itinerant artists.

The Old Lyme Inn offers lodging with an artful past and present.

*The Old Lyme Inn began as a farmhouse in the midst of Connecticut farm country, but the area soon began to sprout as many artists as corn. Some of the Old Lyme paintings are among American Impressionism's best canvases.*

## *Old Lyme Inn*

**85 Lyme Street**
**Old Lyme, CT 06371**
**Reservations: 203/434-2600**

**13 guest rooms. Lunch, dinner, and a light supper are served.**

(Right) *Built-in seating and comfortable Victorian furnishings encourage guests to meet and mingle in the parlor. One conversation piece is the beveled mirror above the fireplace, purchased by the current owner for $5 at a country auction.*

(Below) *The art of the fishing lure is handsomely displayed in a wall panel in the inn's lounge.*

(Above) *Elaborate carvings distinguish this graceful armchair, whose upholstery pattern is typical of the Federal period.*

(Opposite) *Guests who have slept under a golden canopy at the Old Lyme Inn include Hal Holbrook, Robert Redford, and Morley Safer.*

*Two imposing deck chairs wait like soldiers in front of Lake Placid Manor. The lake was the original site of several luxury "camps" built by wealthy New Yorkers seeking to flee the city's summer heat.*

# Lake Placid Manor

## LAKE PLACID, NEW YORK

PETER BOYLE, president of the National Audubon Society, said of New York State's Adirondacks Mountains, "If you spend your time in those hills and you breathe the air and see the trees, it has an impact on your soul."

Many city dwellers over the years have experienced the pleasures of the Adirondacks as guests of the "Great Camps" that serve as summer retreats. In 1882 one of these camps was built on the shores of Lake Placid, amid towering pine trees and in view of Whiteface Mountain.

The camp's rustic lodge changed hands many times. In 1946 the then-new owners added some cottages and a restaurant and named their place Placid Manor.

Finally the facility was purchased by a hotel family from Chicago who now operate it under its current name, Lake Placid Manor.

**STARTED IN 1882**

*The same year that the malted milk was invented by William Horlick of Racine, Wisconsin.*

The lodge, with a stone-and-log facade, still recalls the "Great Camps" of the late 1800s. Each of the guest rooms is decorated in Adirondacks country style and the public rooms feature, among other things, stone and brick fireplaces, a large moose head, and an antique mahogany music box that still plays tunes for guests who drop a nickel in the slot.

The inn takes particular pride in its food. Among the many culinary surprises are eggplant strudel with fontina cheese and fresh basil and rounds of veal stuffed with bacon, artichoke, cheese, and fresh rosemary.

*Spring-fed Lake Placid inspires myriad summer recreational activities, including swimming, but the area is also a cold-weather paradise for sports lovers, having served as the location for two Winter Olympics.*

# Lake Placid Manor

**Lake Placid Manor**
**Whiteface Inn Road**
**Lake Placid, NY 12946**
**Reservations: 518/523-2573**

**30 guest rooms dispersed among the Main Lodge and four outside buildings. All meals are served.**

*The chair in the far right of the living room and the coffee table in the center offer good examples of Adirondack twig furniture. Overlooking this rustic scene from his vantage point on the chimney is a genial moose, who can also be seen in the photo at right.*

(Above) *This stairway was crafted from yellow birch harvested in the nearby mountains. It seems to grow right out of the tree stump.*

(Below, left) *A mirror framed by deer antlers reflects a portion of the dining room. On a clear day diners can view Whiteface Mountain and Kate Smith's former summer home.*

(Below, right) *The guest rooms are furnished and decorated simply in what the owners call "Adirondack country style."*

# The Adelphi Hotel

## SARATOGA SPRINGS, NEW YORK

DIAMOND JIM BRADY, Lillian Russell, and other celebrities participating in Saratoga Springs' summer season had some difficult choices to make each day—whether to visit the world-famous horse racing track, take the waters in one of the spas that initially accounted for the town's popularity as a resort, gamble at the casino, or attend a ball at one of the fashionable hotels along Broadway. Among the latter was the Adelphi.

**BUILT IN 1877**

*The same year that root beer was introduced in America.*

The Adelphi grew up with Saratoga Springs' elegant social life, offering a large piazza overlooking Broadway, ballrooms covered with beautiful draperies, and dozens of pieces of furniture made in the Victorian era.

Today, the hotel still reflects the high style of living during what became known as the Gilded Age. The guest rooms feature high ceilings above ornate Victorian woodwork. Two-room suites are available, with antique furnishings and sitting rooms (including one where Ms. Russell may have once napped). The rooms have been brought into the 20th century with full baths, air conditioning, and cable TV.

Cafe Adelphi has a Victorian bar leading to the same outdoor courtyard and garden that once hosted millionaires discussing the stock market and racetrack favorites. Dinners are served here now in the warm summer months.

Diamond Jim and Lillian Russell are no longer among the summer crowds, but millionaires, celebrities such as Paul Simon and Linda Ronstadt, and just plain folk can be heard extending the same invitation to their friends that many, many previous visitors proffered during the life of this quaint resort town—"Meet me at the Adelphi."

*The facade's white columns and elaborate fretwork provide an appropriate frame for the Lombardian brickwork.*

(Opposite) *The lobby of the Adelphi is a vivid reminder of the Gilded Age when the rich and famous came to Saratoga Springs to "sample the waters" and to play the ponies. Many still do.*

*Diamond Jim Brady and Lillian Russell, frequent visitors at the Adelphi, might well have recognized this trunk-turned-coffee-table, typical of the baggage carted by the large entourages that often accompanied celebrities.*

*The hotel's stairway with its well-turned balustrades and old gilt-framed portraits is lit from above by a skylight.*

**The Adelphi Hotel**
**365 Broadway**
**Saratoga Springs, NY 12866**
**Reservations: 518/587-4688**

34 guest rooms. A continental breakfast featuring homebaked pastries and fresh fruit is delivered to each room every morning and is included in the rates.

(Opposite) *The second floor enables guests to observe strollers and shoppers on Broadway, once the street of many grand-luxe hotels such as the Adelphi.*

# The Edge of Thyme

## Candor, New York

John D. Rockefeller, the founder of the Standard Oil Company and a world-famous philanthropist, did not suffer fools or clerical errors gladly. That is why his private secretary, Rosa Murphy, had to be somewhat of a perfectionist herself.

**STARTED IN 1860**

*The same year that Abraham Lincoln was elected 16th president of the United States.*

At the beginning of the 20th century, Rosa married Dr. Amos Canfield, and she soon lavished her perfectionist tendencies on their home, an old house that she had found and restored in the center of Candor, a small community in the Finger Lakes area of New York. Her creative touches were everywhere, from the leaded glass windows to the marble fireplaces to the parquet floors.

The Canfields' cheerful home has now become an inn. The public rooms are furnished with Queen Anne–style and traditional pieces. The guest rooms are decorated with antiques appropriate to the early 20th century. The bathtubs are those oversized basins prized in 1908 when the home was originally refurbished. Even the showers date from early in the century. The surrounding garden is filled with maples, spruce, flowering crabapple, and dogwood and is accented by a small fish and lily pond.

Breakfast consists of a fruit tart, a cheese fondue entrée, muffins, and coffee or tea. After breakfast, guests can enjoy scenic drives throughout the Finger Lakes and visits to nearby Cornell University, Binghamton, and Cooperstown.

*This handsome white Georgian structure is bracketed by an acre of maples, spruce, dogwood, and flowering crabapples.*

(Opposite) *Rosa Canfield, once private secretary to John D. Rockefeller, decorated her summer retreat with a homespun flair. Seen here is a portion of the breakfast area with leaded glass windows depicting scenes from New England history and a homemade quilt.*

# The Edge of Thyme

The Edge of Thyme
6 Main Street
Candor, NY 13743
Reservations: 800/722-7365

3 guest rooms with private bathrooms, 4 rooms with shared bathrooms. A full breakfast is included in the rates.

*The dining room provides an elegant setting for elegant meals, with highly polished furnishings, silverware, and china.*

*In the evening, guests can gather in the living room and toast the day with a glass of wine. Candor, after all, is located in the heart of New York State's wine country.*

White Adirondack chairs form a conversation circle on the inn's white-columned porch.

Each of the Edge of Thyme's seven guest rooms is decorated with a distinctive mix of antique furnishings. Noteworthy in the room pictured here is the marble-topped dressing table with stained glass insert at left.

An umbrella stand in the foyer holds a trio of old-style bumper shoots and a rustic walking stick.

*Adding to the charm of this dining room corner are the deep-toned wall paneling and the strategically located oil lamps, now converted to electric power.*

# Beekman Arms

## RHINEBECK, NEW YORK

If you were to compile a master list of past guests of the Beekman Arms, you might be dazzled and overwhelmed by the result.

As the oldest continuously operating hotel/tavern in America, the Beekman Arms has attracted:

George Washington, who watched one of his Continental army regiments drill smartly on the front lawn.

Benjamin Harrison, 23rd president of the United States, who was notified of his victory at the polls while staying at the Beekman.

Franklin D. Roosevelt, 32nd president of the United States, who came here often and gave informal talks from the front porch.

And sports and entertainment celebrities ranging from Phil Rizzuto and Joe Louis to Helen Hayes and Brooke Shields.

The building began as Traphagen's Tavern. The doorways were short and wide, to accommodate guests who were not as tall as they are today and women who were wearing hoop skirts in the fashion of the day.

**BUILT IN 1766**

*The same year that Andrew Jackson, seventh president of the United States, was born.*

The public areas are decorated with many traces of the inn's colonial history, such as a framed land deed from 1773, a grandfather clock, and an oil painting of George Washington, and these artifacts are set off by an abundance of exposed old bricks and wood.

The inn today has grown to a complex of five buildings, including (in addition to the original tavern building) a guest house, a carriage house, the Delameter House, the gables, and the Delameter courtyard.

The guest rooms are all furnished with antique items or reproductions of earlier pieces. They also have something George Washington never had while he was staying here.

An electric English pants presser.

*George Washington not only stayed at the Beekman Arms, he reviewed his troops from this very porch.*

(Above) *Celebrities seem drawn to the Beekman's colonial ambience. Kirk Douglas, for example, may have sat on that old church pew before the fireplace, and George Shearing has coaxed a few tunes out of the well-played piano at left.*

*Beekman Arms*

**4 Mill Street**

**Rhinebeck, NY, 12572**

**Reservations: 914/876-7077**

No meals are included in the rates. An antique barn adjacent to the inn offers wares from some 30 dealers.

(Opposite, above) *This stained glass window adds a charming touch to the Tap Room, where guests gather to quaff draft beer and to wrestle with the rustic puzzles that hang on a nearby wall.*

(Opposite, below) *This dining room cupboard features an impressive array of delft containers designed to hold everything from ginger and nutmeg to barley and oatmeal.*

(Above, right) *As this photo shows, four-poster beds for Northeastern homes tended to be rather high off the ground so that sleepers could avoid cold floors during the winter months. The wall picture is a reminder of the nearby Hudson River's steamboating days.*

(Right) *Guests in this Beekman Arms chamber can either sit in the canopy bed and daydream of earlier times or read a book from the selection on the mantel.*

UILT 1684
The Old
Post House
Inn

# *The Old Post House Inn*

## SOUTHAMPTON, NEW YORK

RECENTLY THE MEMBERS of the Suffolk County Archaeological Society Association began a "dig" in the cellar of the Old Post House Inn in Southampton, New York. They uncovered:

17th- and 18th-century bottles.

An 18th-century spoon.

An Indian basket.

Part of an early Bible.

The locals were not too surprised at the age of these relics for the inn is housed in one of the oldest extant wood-frame structures in New York State. When Cecil and Ed Courville, the current innkeepers, began the restoration of the building, they discovered that on every floor a veritable museum of early colonial life awaited them.

In the closets they found large nails made by blacksmiths more than 200 years ago. Parts of the structure are held together with wooden pegs called tree nails, made in the 17th century. Inside a wall was a bottle of Drakes Plantation Bitters, dated 1860. The label reads, "A glassful taken three times a day will impart tone and cheerfulness to the whole system."

**BUILT IN 1684**

*The same year that Spanish conquistadors were establishing their first colonies in Texas.*

Each guest room in this 11-room house is decorated in period style. Many of the structural details, from the 18-inch floorboards to the hand hewn ceiling beams, are remnants of the original 1684 farmhouse.

In addition to the decor, the innkeepers have many colonial-era tales to share with guests, including an unusual occupation of one of the early owners, who it seems, was the first hay warden of Southampton. What is a hay warden? In the 17th century land boundaries were marked by stacks of hay. The warden's job was to see that no greedy landowners increased their acreage by moving the hay a few feet or yards.

*The inn's original 18-inch chestnut floorboards peek out from under the rug in the guest room pictured here. Even more surprises may be hidden in the walls. Indeed, the restoration of the structure revealed a trove of artifacts, from a colonial clay pipe to a bottle of "Drakes Plantation Bitters" dated 1860.*

(Opposite) *Once a precolonial farmhouse, the Post House is still held together in part by wooden pegs called "tree nails."*

(Above) *The Post House parlor is a pleasant winter retreat with a massive brick fireplace ringed by wooden tulips and antique dolls.*

(Left) *Elements of the inn's country decor abound. In the foyer, pictured here, a bright green-and-white color scheme is accented by a vase of freshly picked flowers and a hanging quilt reflected in the mirror.*

**The Old Post House Inn**

**136 Main Street**

**Southampton, NY 11988**

**Reservations: 516/283-1717**

**7 guest rooms. A continental breakfast of croissants and coffee or tea is included in the rates.**

# The Abbey

## Cape May, New Jersey

Residents of Cape May, a resort city on the Atlantic Ocean, are accustomed to seeing amateur photographers pointing their cameras at a Gothic villa with a soaring 60-foot tower. The target of all this picture taking is the Abbey, a wonderful old Victorian house with high arched ruby glass windows. It looks like the perfect place to spend Halloween.

**BUILT IN 1869**

*The same year that John Wesley Powell became the first white American to navigate the Colorado River through the Grand Canyon.*

A father and son were unwittingly responsible for this bed & breakfast complex which actually consists of two Victorian buildings. The first is the main house with the vertigo tower built by John B. McCreary. The other is a home in the Second Empire style—complete with mansard roof—constructed for McCreary's son, George.

Both homes are furnished with High Victorian antiques such as floor to ceiling mirrors, gas lighting fixtures, and marble-topped dressers. All of the guest rooms have private baths. The main house is considered such a milestone in the history of American architecture that scaled drawings of the building are kept in the Library of Congress.

The innkeepers, Jay and Marianne Schatz, are experts at keeping informal conversations going among guests at the "community breakfast." When the talk slows, Jay has been known to liven things up by bringing out one of the 250 hats that he collects. He has everything from top hat to fez.

*Stark white balustrades provide a pleasing counterpoint to the inn's vivid red carpeting, both of which were carefully restored when the building became an inn after a 10-year period of virtual abandonment.*

The 60-foot tower is one of the inn's most distinctive architectural features. Look closely and you will see ruby glass inserts in the structure's arched windows and in those on the third floor.

(Opposite, above right) *In the Newport Room, the simplicity of the white bed and wicker chair is accented by the colorful ceiling border and the Victorian lamps.*

(Opposite, below right) *This carved walnut bed, a genuine Victorian antique, reflects the type of elegance that led many early-20th-century visitors to call Cape May the "Queen of the Seaside Resorts."*

*The Abbey*

**Columbia Avenue & Gurney Street**
**Cape May, NJ 08204**
**Reservations: 609/884-4506**

14 guest rooms in two side-by-side buildings. A breakfast (a full meal in spring and fall and a continental buffet in summer) is included in the rates.

(Above) *No doubt Queen Victoria herself would have felt perfectly at home in this parlor, which is crowded with "Victoriana," from the arched draped doorway to the shimmering crystal chandelier.*

102
Vacancy

# The Queen Victoria

## Cape May, New Jersey

The Cape May Peninsula on the tip of New Jersey is shaped like a finger pointing right at Delaware, with one of the oldest resort towns in America, also named Cape May, right about at the fingernail. There are so many Victorian buildings here that the whole town has been declared a National Historic Landmark.

**BUILT IN 1882**

*The same year that Jesse James was shot in the back in his St. Joseph, Missouri, home by Robert Ford.*

Few buildings epitomize the Victorian era better than the Queen Victoria inn. This three-story mansion rising just a block from the ocean is a riot of Victorian architectural clichés, with cupolas, wide porches, and dormer windows.

Small wonder that the Queen Victoria has been a "cover girl" for a wide variety of companies and publications. Sherwin-Williams used the house to illustrate its Victorian paints. The U.S. Department of Commerce featured the Queen Victoria on its foreign travel brochure, "America—Catch the Spirit." *McCall's* selected the inn as one of its 100 recommended destinations for "getting away from it all."

The inn traces its origins to 1881 when a Delaware River pilot purchased a plot of land in Cape May for $3,500, and spent another $4,000 to construct the house of his extravagant dreams. After the pilot died, the house passed through a series of owners and uses.

Dane and Joan Wells purchased the property in 1980 and spent several years removing the detritus of decades, restoring many of the original room configurations, and removing the aging white and green exterior paint (possibly to the great relief of Sherwin-Williams).

Today you can settle into the Prince of Wales Room, the Oscar Wilde Room, or the Dickens Room, just a few of the 24 elegantly named and decorated rooms and suites scattered throughout the inn complex. Some modern touches have been added for the guests' enjoyment, such as a player piano in the parlor, refrigerators to chill wines, and even a popcorn popper next to an inviting mound of unpopped corn.

*A blue rocker peeks through a pink porch fence that is a riot of circles and oblong spaces.*

(Opposite) *This splendid example of Victorian architecture cost $4,000 to build in 1878. The land cost $500 less.*

**The Queen Victoria**
**102 Ocean Street**
**Cape May, NJ 08204**
**Reservations: 609/884-8702**

**24 rooms and suites in three buildings in the Historic Landmark area. A full breakfast is included in the rates.**

(Opposite) *The bay-windowed parlor seen here occupies a portion of the turret that gives the building its distinctive shape. A nearby player piano and log fire provide winter diversions. In summer guests head for the nearby beach.*

(Above) *White wicker chairs and sofas with bright yellow cushions add a light airy feeling to this main house suite. Look closely at the antique framed cards on the wall. They portray characters from Gilbert & Sullivan operas and were once given away as premiums by a cigarette company.*

(Left) *The dining room table is ready for a help-yourself buffet breakfast that includes home granola and egg casserole dishes. Late risers can elect to have breakfast in bed.*

(Below) *Mythical griffins guard a beautiful ebonized chair that dates from the turn-of-the-century Aesthetic period.*

# Longswamp Bed & Breakfast

## MERTZTOWN, PENNSYLVANIA

THE UNDERGROUND RAILROAD was a pre–Civil War phenomenon that helped former slaves gain their freedom by shuttling them, often under cover of darkness, to various "stations" on the way to Northern states and Canada.

**STARTED CIRCA 1792**

*The same period that saw the laying of the cornerstone of the U.S. Capitol building in Washington, D. C.*

One of these stations was a small cottage next to a large farmhouse located on 50 acres in Pennsylvania. A tunnel to the cottage helped facilitate the secret comings and goings of the runaways and their helpers. Later, the cottage became the local post office and general store and the farmhouse became the Longswamp Bed & Breakfast inn.

The historic farmhouse is typical of many such structures built in the late 18th century. It is close to Amish country and surrounded by orchards, old maple trees, and many flowering shrubs and wildflowers. Each of the guest rooms is furnished in an "eclectic" style with antiques. Many floral papers and fabrics are used in the room decorations. The guest rooms are located in the main house as well as in the cottage, now converted from an Underground Railroad station to a comfortable weekend hideaway with exposed original ceiling beams, a skylight, and a stone fireplace.

The owners and innkeepers are Elsa and Dean Dimick. Elsa is a professional cook and takes special pride in preparing seasonal breakfasts for her guests. These might include orange juice, pumpkin waffles with cider syrup and poached apple slices, served with country bacon and "lots of coffee." Elsa gets her beans for the coffee directly from New Orleans and grinds them to order.

Active guests can play basketball in the barn, pitch horseshoes, or have a volleyball game. Loaner bikes are available to those who would like to pedal through the countryside where nighttime freedom-seekers once trod.

*This 14-room mansion, which took 25 years to complete, served a dramatic role in the days before the Civil War—it was a station on the Underground Railroad that helped Southern slaves flee north to freedom.*

(Opposite) *This parlor table appears ready for an afternoon card game or a spot of tea.*

(Above, left) *This toy rocking horse, once the delight of a young resident of the mansion, now rides the fireplace mantel in the parlor.*

(Above, right) *Longswamp proprietors Elsa and Dean Dimick have spent a lifetime collecting memorabilia. Here are a few of their treasures in the guest room named "Rachel's."*

*A library and stained glass windows add unusual touches to the breakfast room where the hostess serves such morning surprises as pumpkin waffles topped with cider sauce and poached apple slices.*

*Longswamp Bed & Breakfast*
**RD 2, Box 26**
**Mertztown, PA 19539**
**Reservations: 215/682-6197**

**6 guest rooms in the main house with additional accommodations in the adjacent cottage. A full country breakfast is included in the rates.**

# Cameron Estate Inn

## Mount Joy, Pennsylvania

If the walls of the Cameron Estate Inn could only talk, what historic anecdotes they might recount.

Perhaps they could tell us why Mr. Simon Cameron helped turn the tide in favor of Abraham Lincoln at the Republican Convention in 1860.

**BUILT IN 1805**

*The same year that saw the Lewis and Clark expedition reach the northern fringe of the American frontier.*

Or perhaps they could tell us what the early days of the Civil War were really like.

Even though the inn's walls are silent, Simon Cameron's dinner conversations must have been filled with such revelations. He was a long-time power broker in Pennsylvania politics, and he influenced national elections. He commanded the War Department during the first months of the Civil War (although some said he was too free with the country's treasury) and was U.S. Ambassador to Russia.

You would expect such a man to choose a monumental house for his private home and late in his life he did just that. It was a three-story red-brick Federal-style building in Donegal Springs, Pennsylvania, an imposing edifice that had been built originally for John Watson, the great-grandfather of President William McKinley. Mr. Cameron celebrated the purchase of the home by planting hundreds of shade trees and shrubs on the grounds. Two trout streams that met in front of the porch completed the bucolic scene.

In 1981 it was Abe and Betty Groff's turn to be enchanted by the mansion. They owned the nearby Groff's Farm Restaurant and reasoned that the Cameron estate would make a wonderful inn. They have completely restored the building and added fine Colonial and Federal-style furnishings to the decor. The guest rooms have been furnished with high poster, canopied, or brass beds. The Groffs have kept the original wide-plank floors and the working fireplaces.

French and American country cuisine is served at dinner. And sometimes on still nights when the waiter brings you such appetizers as crab-stuffed mushrooms, you may even think you hear a faint snatch of conversation.

"About your vote at the Republican convention . . ."

*Antique bottles on a mantelpiece reflect Lancaster County's long history. Near the site of the inn, for example, the congregation of Donegal Church gathered in 1777 to pledge allegiance to the new nation.*

*Cameron Estate Inn*
**Donegal Springs Road**
**RD 1, Box 305**
**Mount Joy, PA 17552**
**Reservations: 717/653-1773**

**18 guest rooms, 16 with a private bath or shower. Breakfast is included in the rate. Lunch and dinner are also served.**

(Opposite, above left) *In this handsome room one can almost see Simon Cameron, Lincoln's first Secretary of War, huddled with his guests over conversation and brandy. Note the politically correct portrait over the mantel.*

(Opposite, below left) *This loft bedchamber is one of 18 guest rooms at the inn. The handsome but simply colored quilt on the bed is a reminder that the inn is located in Amish country.*

(Below) *White lawn chairs beckon guests to relax after a day of hiking the 15-acre property. Two trout streams are a fly-cast away.*

(Right) *Many of the guest rooms are furnished with reproduction and antique Federal pieces. Blue, so popular in colonial homes, is the predominant color here, enriching the rug, the fireplace, and the canopied bed.*

# The Bechtel Mansion Inn

## East Berlin, Pennsylvania

Queen Victoria ruled England for 64 years, from 1837 to 1901. Her gentle, refined reign defined an entire era of manners, architecture, and interior design. Appropriately, it became known as the Victorian age.

Today Queen Victoria would probably feel right at home at the Bechtel Mansion Inn, a bright yellow Victorian house that is a treasure trove of that era's furniture and design.

Here are a few examples:

The parlor downstairs is decorated with the mansion's original Brussels carpet and the original 1897 wallpaper.

Light in the dining room comes from etched glass windows that illuminate a large window seat and a built-in corner cupboard of oak.

One of the showpieces of the living room is an early 19th-century oak secretary with mahogany inlay.

The master bedroom has a magnificent built-in oak wardrobe with a full-length mirror and a special clock shelf.

**BUILT IN 1897**

*The same year that the first American subway began to operate in Boston. Its route was 1.8 miles long.*

The chandeliers throughout the inn are from the original mansion, which was built for William G. Leas, the wealthiest man in East Berlin. The home remained in the Leas family until 1982, when it was sold at public auction to Charles Bechtel. Thereafter Bechtel began converting the building to an inn.

In addition to the many period touches inside, the inn also features a typical 19th-century-style garden with displays of daffodils, peonies, tulips, and sweet william.

The Bechtel Mansion Inn is located in the center of the tiny town of East Berlin, which features numerous buildings that have been preserved for more than 100 years. The town was originally called Berlin by German immigrants, but when the U.S. Postal Service was formed, "East" was added to distinguish the town from another Berlin in the same state.

*Meals at the Bechtel Mansion Inn are quiet, elegant affairs served on old china under a brass chandelier.*

(Opposite) *This Queen Anne-style mansion on West King and Fourth Street was built in 1897. Some years before both Union and Confederate soldiers had trod the ground on which the inn now stands on their way to Gettysburg.*

THE
LEAS-BECHTEL
MANSION
INN
BED AND
BREAKFAST

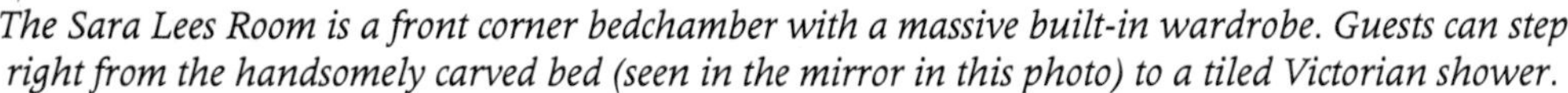

*The Sara Lees Room is a front corner bedchamber with a massive built-in wardrobe. Guests can step right from the handsomely carved bed (seen in the mirror in this photo) to a tiled Victorian shower.*

(Right) *The Master Bedroom is the first choice of many honeymoon couples. The restored carpet is original to the mansion, and the walnut queen-size bed displays a handsome Lone Star-patterned quilt.*

(Above, center) *A movie depicting late-19th-century life could be filmed in this Victorian parlor without replacing a single item. The horsehair-upholstered furniture and the original Brussels carpet and wallpaper are remarkably true to the era.*

(Opposite, below right) *Beautiful polished woods and elegantly turned balustrades create a dramatic staircase at the Bechtel Mansion Inn, part of a meticulous restoration that has continued on the site since 1933.*

*Etched glass panes and elaborate carved details on the double front doors welcome guests to the Bechtel Mansion Inn, one of the 15 properties of the East Berlin Historic District.*

The Bechtel Mansion Inn
400 West King Street
East Berlin, PA 17316
Reservations: 717/259-7760

9 guest rooms, plus 2 additional rooms in a carriage house on the property. A deluxe continental breakfast (homebaked coffee cakes, fruit ambrosia, cheese, and apple butter) is included in the rates.

76
Robert
Morris
Inn
OPEN

# The Robert Morris Inn

## Oxford, Maryland

Early in the 18th century British ships bobbing across the Atlantic toward Oxford, Maryland—then the colony's principal port of entry—carried many of the materials that would be used in the construction of a home in Oxford for Robert Morris, Sr.

**BUILT IN 1710**

*During the period when high heels and curled wigs became the rage for both men and women.*

Ships' nails and wooden pegs were used as joiners while bricks—ballast from deep in the bellies of the ships—became the source material for fireplaces and walls. Even the ships' carpenters were pressed into shore duty on behalf of the Morris' home.

In 1738 Robert Morris, Sr. arrived from England and moved into the home. He was joined several years later by his son, Robert Morris, Jr., who would one day help finance the American Revolution. Robert Morris, Jr. also became a signer of the American Declaration of Independence and raised money that helped support George Washington's army in the field.

In the 1940s the Morris home was converted into a country inn. Some years later Ken and Wendy Gibson became the innkeepers. They preserved many of the early architectural features, even the slightly slanted floorboards, the Elizabethan-style enclosed staircase, and the wall murals made from 140-year-old wallpaper. Rather than add more guest rooms by enlarging the home, they began to purchase nearby houses and converted them to additional sleeping quarters.

The dining room in the main residence still retains much of its early charm, with an open fireplace and a slate floor. The house specialty is unquestionably crab cakes ("backfin crabmeat combined with our own special seasonings, lightly breaded and fried"). For diners who are concerned about fat and calories in their foods, the inn also serves the crab cakes oven-baked, without breading.

Guests can stroll and antique shop in the small town of Oxford or sit on the inn porch with a good view of the red Avon River, the transportation artery that once brought ashore many of the raw materials that went into the making of the Robert Morris Inn.

*"Oxford" crab cakes are the specialty of the house, perhaps sampled here by an impressive roster of stellar visitors over the years, including Bing Crosby, Elizabeth Taylor, and Robert Mitchum.*

(Opposite) *A 1776 flag proudly heralds the American Revolution, an event that ironically signalled the economic downturn of the inn's hometown, Oxford, Maryland.*

*The Riverview Room, painted a bright Williamsburg blue, is a favorite gathering place for guests of the Robert Morris Inn. The brick used to line the fireplace once served as ballast on sailing ships from England.*

(Previous pages) *A row of benches on the long front porch offers guests a view of the peaceful red Avon River.*

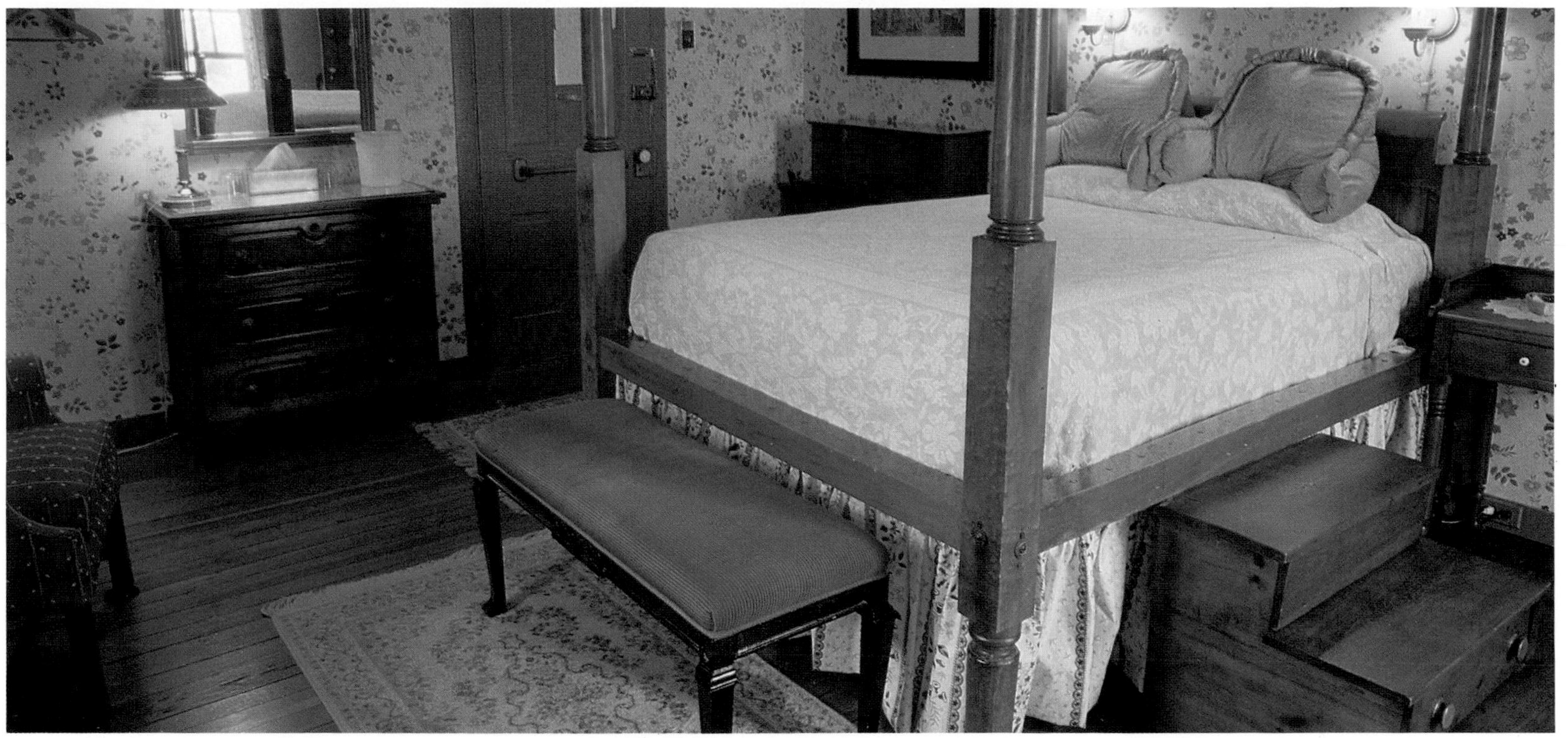

*A handy wooden stairs helps people clamber into the high four-poster bed in the third floor guest room.*

The Robert Morris Inn
**Box 70**
**Oxford, MD 21654**
**Reservations: 301/226-5111**

30 guest rooms with private baths, 3 with shared baths. A family apartment is also available. All meals are served.

*A decorative wooden screen masks a fireplace opening in the Riverview Room. Perhaps these painted waterfowl remind visitors of the "Strand," a nearby beach, where feeding real ducks is a popular pastime.*

# Acknowledgment

The producers of *Historic Inns of the Northeast* gratefully acknowledge the assistance of the innkeepers whose fine lodging places are the subject of this book.